Contents

Leadership Calls for Time Management 4

What Causes Poor Time Management 12

Procrastination 16

Realizing Your Present Productivity 24

How to Prevent Disasters 30

Learn to Delegate 33

Time Management Techniques 36

Avoid Interruptions 47

Prioritizing 52

Tips to Help You Prioritize 59

Tips for Staying Focused 66

Work Less Accomplish More 71

Using Affirmations 79

Conclusion 85

Leadership Calls for Time Management

Outline

A decent time supervisor is moreover thought to be an awesome pioneer. Why? Since they step toward achieving objectives for their business. They glance around and find things and zones that need tweaking and apply standards toward influencing them to work.

An incredible time chief similarly knows how to lead and spur other individuals in finding originative approaches to improve utilization of their chance. They show others how its done and are free with their help and information.

As pioneers, they unendingly share ways, tips and procedures on improving as a chief of time, conditions of undertakings and conditions.

Administration

Running business online requires the business visionary to be a successful chief of their chance, empowering them to catch a few ventures or organizations at one time, and, having the capacity to oversee them all in an effective manner.

The net business visionary can't appreciate any of their concern achievement on the off chance that they're dropping off clients, coming up short on time - not having the capacity to charge their clients for that time, or unfit to finish their tasks.

Having the capacity to effectively deal with ventures is among the key pointers of a domestic venture enterpriser who deals with their opportunity well. Do they oversee by emergencies or by aim? Is it a player in their objective to go either gradually or rapidly in venture administration, pointing toward a needed outcome?

The influence this may have on the work from home business visionary effects any potential succeeding business and may in like manner pollute their net notoriety. The greater part of this is tied into appropriate and viable time administration! Is there a response for this obstacle?

Time = Management

Overseeing time successfully is possibly the number 1 objective of practically every work at home enterpriser on their journey for progress. Without having powerful time administration, their net organizations endure despairingly.

Making originative use of their chance is the objective of practically every work at home enterpriser who wishes to be effective in their home

organizations. Successful time administration will give the work at home business person a chance to have the capacity to accomplish more with their opportunity and have satisfied purchasers and a very much settled business.

Viable time administration requires a decided scope of aptitudes, methodologies and devices and enables the net business person to utilize them keeping in mind the end goal to accomplish specific assignments, tasks and objectives. Without the vital use of their opportunity, they're fundamentally squandering their chance and unfit to finish essential business objectives.

It's extremely essential for the net business person to viably oversee time in their household venture for a great deal of reasons:

- They may finish extends in an opportune way

On the off chance that they're ready to be successful in completing undertakings, they may go up against more work; more representatives and better satisfy their customer stacks by productively meeting due dates.

- They're better ready to make quality work

Greater quality work comes about when there's additional time and more thoughtfulness regarding particulars given to the work. Quality work may just be a consequence of watchful tending and meticulousness to detail.

- They may secure more work as they're ready to meet due dates

As a work at home enterpriser, meeting due dates for your clients resembles ensured work! For all intents and purposes everything on the Net is time-touchy so when you're ready to meet due dates, you demonstrate that you're answerable and focused on the main job.

- R.O.I.

There's a considerable rate of profitability with consideration regarding particulars in the household undertaking of the business person once they may successfully deal with their chance. In the event that they may accomplish more over the span of a traverse of time, they diminish the measure of time to land the position achieved, yet are as yet ready to make the same, if not more money.

The arrival on their venture (arranging time) is incredible!

- Gratification

There's a general sentiment satisfaction and accomplishment when the online business person finishes an errand. The sentiment consummation goes about as a helper and gives him or her inventive start they require to either approach a crisp client or mix up more business with old clients.

These components are regularly helpers for the work at home enterpriser to deal with their opportunity well and find originative approaches to work all the more effectively. It's normally the little points of interest of maintaining a business (like overseeing time) that assistance the business visionary follow through on his business matters.

All the same, there are not generally great circumstances or straightforward circumstances when all runs well with the business visionary who endeavors to complete a ton of things over the span of their business relations. When they're in charge of each period of their business, there's dependably the capability of disappointment or dissatisfaction for absence of arranging or sorting out.

What happens when time administration doesn't function admirably or create the needed outcomes?

Are altogether net business visionaries tested regarding the matter of time administration?

There are times that the work from home enterpriser finds that their frameworks and systems aren't working. They find that in any case what they do, they can't stay centered and complete the errands or objectives that they have. They find that they're essentially ineffectively dealing with their opportunity and unfit to achieve neither little nor enormous objectives.

What might be the culprit? Poor administration of time.

What Causes Poor Time Management

Outline

Below average time administration - does the net business person ever trust that he has poor time administration? Or then again, does he consequently trust that he's dealing with his chance proficiently and viably just on the grounds that he's an entrepreneur?

In any case, he needs to circumspectly prepare for sitting around idly or not boosting the full use of the adaptable time that work at home business people have. Without a self-stating exertion, he might be destined for inadequacy or simply business disappointment.

Much of the time, lingering is the essential culprit of poor time administration, yet is as often as possible not considered as important as of the

seen "imagination" in pausing. Put in an unexpected way, net business people much of the time have anxiety about moving too quick on business tasks or settling on choices too quickly.

As honorable as this may sound, it might regularly have the contrary impact and make the work from home individual move too gradually, move too quick or do nothing by any stretch of the imagination. Great time administration may help.

What Harms Time Management

Neglecting to design in any household undertaking isn't not the same as neglecting to design in some other kind of business. There must be a plan of action figured, an advertising methodology took after out and an arrangement of activity to achieve objectives for the business. This all binds into the capacity to configuration, viably handle time and assets and finding what works for the business.

Arranging day by day may appear like a ton of work to do yet in genuine truth when it turns into a propensity, it gets the chance to be second nature. Studies demonstrate that it takes a normal of twenty-one times for a remark to be a propensity. When something gets to be a propensity, it's significantly less difficult to keep up than if it's new or from the earliest starting point.

Home business people have add up to adaptability and accommodation in their occupations. There's nobody remaining over them, requesting their day, revealing to them what to achieve, when to achieve it, how to achieve it, et cetera. With the majority of this flexibility, an undisciplined individual won't see how to viably deal with their chance or when to state no to specific activities or crisp business.

For a ton of business people, they put off their work obligations or commitments for boundless reasons. Doing this may cause unfathomable pressure for the business person and make them handle or work in an emergencies mode.

Working in that way may deliver extra issues that may turn out to be difficult to illuminate or oversee. There are mistakes made, uncompleted undertakings, missed objectives, inferior work quality and even below average business comes about.

Procrastination

Rundown

What are a couple of the real reasons why home business people falter?

Can any anyone explain why they put off touching base at choices, starting crisp tasks, seeking after new business or notwithstanding finishing enormous activities that have affect on more business for them?

We should take a couple of reasons why:

Dawdle

- The net business person has below average work propensities

The work at home enterpriser who has below average work propensities is regularly moderate beginning at everything. They're constant slackers and set aside long stretches of opportunity to complete undertakings or get anything achieved.

- What may come about because of this kind of net business movement?

Thrashing and misfortune in business and deals. In the event that they miss a due date or they neglect to speak with their purchasers or customers that may bring about lost business and a harming perspective of their net notoriety.

This isn't useful for any eventual net and web business person.

Frequently, they similarly hesitate on everything else in their lives, including individual locales, and are always endeavoring to "make up for lost time". This invigorates high strain levels and low creation levels.

The net business person who has below average work propensities is moreover under the feeling that they execute better under strain. Not honest.

They feel that they may do their best work in the event that they're compelled to work snappier, initiating their inventiveness. Not honest. What the majority of this does is just place them promote behind in their work and cause more pressure. Period.

- They've consistent sentiments of being overwhelmed

The net business person who's tested in the region of compelling time administration every now and again feels like they never have anything accomplished. They every now and again don't do anything at all in response to either being proactive in their work or in finishing undertakings.

The overwhelming inclination may likewise prompt uneasiness and the penchant to make tremendous, costly blunders in their work. It's for the most part realized that when you're worn out or overpowered, the limit and plausibility of influencing blunders to step ups exponentially. Normally, this adds significantly more to the sentiment being overmastered and feeling under-achieved.

There's in like manner a sentiment futility in business ventures with enterprisers who hesitate. They feel like it may be less demanding to do nothing at all due to the sheer size of what their endeavor is. This indeed is cyclic and may actuate a winding impact in the business. Since one thing doesn't get expert, it makes an alternate thing not get refined and the procedure may proceed and may cause significantly more issues.

- They feel that they should be "great"

This is possibly among the most widely recognized however most harming identity qualities that a work from home enterpriser has. To a blame, they feel that they should be impeccable, keep away from all blunders no matter what, get things amend the first run through and have the capacity to absolutely and distinctly fulfill the client's each motivation and need. It isn't just farfetched to trust this, however it's in like manner harming and out of line for the business visionary to expect if of himself.

Expecting compulsiveness is a bogus conviction of the net business person. It is extremely unlikely that they might be immaculate, and they put undue strain on themselves thusly.

They wish to complete tasks, meet due dates, accomplish objectives and do them all at record speed! Be that as it may, what keeps them down is as often as possible just going ahead.

They may see their business extends as saddling and disregard them as unimportant. This much of the time improves them feel as they're ready to persuade themselves that on the off chance that they're not urgent, at that point it may be similarly as inconsequential to their customers or purchasers. The business person will regularly put off consummation till the undertaking meets their measures for flawlessness.

In spite of the fact that this percept is just valued by the enterpriser, these principles are much of the time not perceived by their clients.

This normally strengthens the way that it's a period waster and they've worked unbeneficially towards a superfluous end.

- The business person is apathetic

Nonchalant? Do work at home enterprisers genuinely get exhausted? Absolutely they do! Be that as it may, not in the sense where repetitiveness is every now and again used.

They get mundane with no inventiveness or change in their work. Despite the fact that they may maybe adore what they do, they find that doing likewise all the live long day winds up uninteresting and non-trying for them. Along these lines, their fatigue sets in and they lose enthusiasm for the ventures that they're dealing with.

A great deal of times, the work at home individual would only rather be accomplishing something unique other than working. Does that mean they're apathetic? Hardly! They every now and again simply don't comprehend where to start or how to deal with their business activities or how to kick off something in their business to get their interests.

They may look for other originative outlets that are not business related, such as drawing in on social locales or group exchange sheets instead of extremely working. Ordinary assignments like printed material or net occupations may overshadow truly doing work.

The business person will simply continue putting assignments off, wishing they'd either mysteriously turned out to be shorter or vanish. Their strain level may expand, realizing that this endeavor will undoubtedly not occur, and may make their occupations harder to accomplish and objectives harder to figure it out.

What are the aftereffects of these catches? Do you hone compelling time administration?

Realizing Your Present Productivity

Summary

Here are a couple of issues to tolerate as a primary concern that may radically influence your efficiency rate with regards to your business:

What's Happening Now

- Beginning your day with no activity design

On the off chance that you start your day with no activity design, you're cursed from the begin! You begin off late and feel overwhelmed from the earliest starting point. You at that point spend your day in a guarded and emergency mind-set.

You may similarly get yourself swiftly and self-assertively reacting to other individuals' issues and occasions and place them higher up than your own issues.

- No balance

There are 7 enter regions in our lives where we need to hone harmony keeping in mind the end goal to feel and have achievement:

Wellness - how your body feels and how it responds to outside stimulants

Loved ones - quality time and obligations with friends and family

Financial - measure of financial weights and income commitments

Intellectual - how outside stimulants influence your life

Social - how you connect with other individuals

Professional - the techniques that you use to propel your vocation

Spiritual - your association with the higher power and other individuals

Every one of these zones requires our day by day time for fulfillment, in spite of the fact that they may not all get equivalent time each day. It's not all that pivotal to invest critical energy in each territory, yet it's essential to invest a brief period in each region.

In the whole deal, our lives will be adjusted and amicable on the off chance that we spend an adequate sum and nature of time in each region. All the same, on the off chance that we neglect any of these regions, we may rapidly disrupt our prosperity.

For instance, on the off chance that we don't deal with our wellbeing, our friends and family and social life endure. In like manner, in case we're out of adjust in our money related assets, we can't enough fixate on our expert objectives, vocation dreams and extra essential regions of core interest.

- Cluttered up workspace

A jumbled up workspace may create a jumbled up work brain.

Issues result when you can't discover critical business archives or find information for your clients. These things incite pandemonium, wreak madhouse and disarray, however may similarly prompt lost income and deferred charging.

Studies have been directed, demonstrating that a person who works with a jumbled up work area spends around one to two hours daily hunting down things or being occupied by them. This may include altogether in hours misused every week.

- Poor rest

The culprit of poor rest is the fault for a ton of net business visionaries not meeting objectives or getting brings about their organizations. Insufficient rest may prompt terrible quality choices or unreasonable determinations as they identify with pivotal business capacities.

Studies have prove that almost 75% of net enterprisers are restless, and that their organizations are accidentally affected. Being worn out isn't great or beneficial for the work at home person.

In the event that the insufficiency of rest doesn't contrarily affect the business person, the gauge of their rest will. This infers when they do get the opportunity to rest, it's normally erratic, eager rest in view of crucial pressure and other crippling parts.

Stress-filled days are risky to the net business person and may in the long run end up adverse. The key is to sufficiently secure rest and legitimate rest to encounter less pressure and turn out to be more profitable.

- Not taking breaks

Taking average breaks and continuous breaks is a major disappointment of the net business person.

Since they're not on a standard or unbending calendar as in a corporate scene, they feel that they shouldn't need to or can't think about breaks. They may similarly feel that doing as such is an exercise in futility. Not honest. Taking adequate breaks is crucial to day by day triumphs.

A considerable measure of times, the net business visionary in like manner fails to take adequate breaks as they feel just as they may create better outcomes.

They feel that in the event that they work straight through, that they may get more expert and be more beneficial. This doesn't create more outcomes or far and away superior work time.

On the off chance that the body is depleted, response and imagination are gravely hampered and may make the nature of the business person's work endure.

How to Prevent Disasters

Summary

Observe the ways you can keep debacles from happening.

Do It Right

- Produce plans that work

To improve use of your chance in your household venture, create plans that stream and function admirably inside your work space. Systematize and compose stuff so that there's a strategy that leads one stage to work with the following stage et cetera et cetera. Try not to start over each time you need to deliver something.

- Produce plans to address redundant occupations

This would incorporate any paper as well as advanced innovation that you'd use to take care of business in your business. Always have enough supplies accessible that you can promptly get at.

Use a timetable, computerized or paper, to monitor arrangements. You can perceive what, wear and when you need to do what consistently, initially. This may help you effectively design your day for ideal outcomes.

Always work with a spotless work area, with papers recorded and composed and perpetually have the most every now and again used things for your business in your quick handle.

- Plan enough rest periods

Rest experts prescribe for the typical, solid adult to get no less than eight hours of rest a night. This encourages them to work adequately and be extremely gainful, yet a survey by the National Sleep Foundation's 2000 Sleep in America omnibus survey found that, on the normal, adults rest just shy of seven hours amid the work week.

As an enterpriser, you should plan an adequate measure of rest for ideal profitability. The sum is diverse for every one of us and you should give your body a chance to perceive what conditions it works best under.

Some require 8 hours, some more, others less. Your body perceives the appropriate response.

- Formulate Your imparting aptitudes

Your capacity to apropos and unhesitatingly impart what you comprehend both orally and in composing is amazingly urgent to your business' prosperity. Gain it an in ground sense of duty regarding keep on bettering your talking and composing aptitudes. You'll spare time and have a more effective employment.

Learn to Delegate

Abstract

Delegation is immensely imperative to time administration. The capacity to effectively assign permits you as a net business visionary the flexibility to take a shot at extra ventures.

Know When To Turn It Over

To upgrade your chance, make sure to orchestrate a reasonable and reachable due date for any assigned work that you administer. Verify that the appointment is reasonable and adjusted and is workable for the person to whom you allocated to. Continuously be specific about what you need done when you appoint work in order to keep any disarray and to verify that you achieve the coveted results important.

When assigning, be extremely obvious about the reason for the work that you're designating and what kind of results you expect.

Be careful with designating without headings, as it might cause chaos, confuse and inferior work quality. In the event that you do not have an opportunity to give the individual finish and express bearings, you may wish to give the work to a person who may make do with little communication from you. This will keep you from smaller scale overseeing and free you up to be more profitable.

Continuously let the person to whom you appointed be originative in their work. Just look for and expect quality results without managing well ordered on how the venture is to be executed. This kills your entire motivation behind designating and may similarly cause undue pressure.

Devise a plan to report back to you to get criticism on the person's advance. This shields you from being never-endingly

disturbed amid the day. Keep a rundown of key dates with the goal that you get the input all the time. Make a point to similarly keep a log of all your assigned activities and refresh the log as you secure criticism.

Time Management Techniques

Summary

Use these strategies to deal with your time better.

Oversee It Better

- Preparation

Approach time to set no less than 10 minutes each night to plan the next day. You should typically plan around 60-70% of your opportunity to take into consideration interruptions and crises. Draw from your rundown of things that are high need and orchestrate squares of time where you work at a specific zone of your business.

- Organize

Set aside the opportunity to compose your office by class. Do this by putting the greater part of your appropriate records and information that relates together in one place.

Put the greater part of your money related printed material together. Put the majority of your monetary related issues together. This will enable you to focus on one anticipate at once and be an invited help. Coordinate your office notwithstanding organizing your chance. Usage records to keep yourself focused and on track. Being sorted out is a consistent technique.

Spending two or three hours sorting out yourself now will spare you 100s of hours in an opportunity to come.

- File Systems

An incredible recording and printed material framework will give you a chance to be exceptionally beneficial. Set your documents to mirror the accompanying things:

- To achieve

Normally, this would hold everything that you plan to achieve or have achieved on an occasional premise, regardless of whether that is each day,

consistently, every quarter or consistently. Compact to achieve records are imperative to the accomplishment of the household venture individual. You should and may in like manner record any old to achieve records in the wake of having completed them. This will give you chronicled information and referencing in the event that you need to backpedal and look for customer or undertaking data.

- To think about

There isn't sufficient time in the business visionary's day to examine the majority of the messages, postal mail material, magazines, ebooks and indexes that run over his work area or PC. When you've data that is originating from a considerable measure of sources both on the web and disconnected, you must be sure to keep them sorted out for future reference. Record this material for future auditing and contemplating when additional time is admissible.

Keep a tickler record on the web and disconnected so you can without much of a stretch access them both voluntarily. Especially in instances of net recording, you can complete a few issues to better deal with your opportunity.

1.) Sort your mail into a computerized organizer with a mark. Makes it easier to discover for future access.

2.) Upload it to your email inbox or email supplier.

3.) Transfer the organizer to your PDA or extra innovative gadgets

4.) Later or if time licenses, see the correspondence and either an.) Erase it or b.) to follow up on it

- Thoughts

Use the musings organizer to hold your originative contemplations and any future considerations you have for the business. This may similarly be a piece of your objectives and objective setting, yet should hold innovative reasoning considerations and sparkles. You can in like manner use this organizer to hold extra thoughts or showcasing procedures that you chance upon. This is to set the phase to start more contemplations inside you when you survey the organizer. This organizer can possibly develop fundamentally as a major piece of any household undertaking is advancing, advancing, advancing.

- Resolutions

This envelope will bear resolutions to either correspondence that you've sent to likely or show clients or answers that you're accommodating yourself. Don't know the amount you charged for that last venture you improved the situation X Customer? Look in the resolutions organizer. Shouldn't something be said about the statement that you gave the net telephone catalog organization after they got some information about your telecom administrations... it might just be in the resolutions envelope. Resolutions might be in light of inquiries that you've conveyed or have gotten into your office.

- References

The reference organizer is fundamental to your business and aides massively with promoting endeavors. You should have correspondence that is referrals for going before employments and letters of proposals in that organizer. The reference organizer should (and may) similarly hold references that you require for different sorts of ventures where another individual is required. Put in an unexpected way, in the event that you are a substance creator yet need to discover a website specialist, look in your reference organizer and see who

suggests whom as that. This might be an invaluable bit of time administration and authoritative device for your business. Augment its use by recording and archiving germane and applicable information that is profoundly focused to specific specialty territories.

- Copies

Everything that stumbles upon your work area should be duplicated in some way. That incorporates buy receipts, contracts, charges, assess information, customer work orders and any and everything that relates to your business. Keeping in mind the end goal to decrease the measure of messiness this may cause, carefully duplicate everything and store it on your PC or on a go down plate. Simply, examine archives into your PC and spare it to a predefined territory. This makes it considerably more straightforward to review it when you require it.

- File

Entirely clear as crystal, this tickler record is for everything that must be documented. Build up a plan that is easy to recall and removes the speculating from "where may it be?" This framework will give you a chance to discover the information that you need when you need it, keeping it out of your route and off of your work area.

- PC

Figure out how to use your PC viably and productively. Find approaches to take full preferred standpoint of it and amplify its usage for your business. Put resources into courses or if nothing else purchase how-to books for each program in your framework. Your PC may make your days more beneficial and streamlined toward powerful time administration if it's

legitimately used. Learning it in its totality and the various highlights that it has will enable you to improve use of your chance.

- Creative reasoning

Innovative reasoning is the start and spine of any fruitful net business. Without it, thoughts can't take shape and organizations can't be framed. A mind that is casual, calm and cheerful is more helpful for sparkles and episodes of innovative reasoning and has more opportunity to fixate completely on accomplishing great business. Invest originative energy considering, perusing and investigating ways and considerations that may enhance your business. Little bits of time on an everyday premise may help and result in viable methods.

- Preparation

Day by day arrangement the prior night work the following day creates a synchronized framework to help you in your business. An extraordinary arrangement can't be discretionarily fudged together yet must be carefully composed.

Without an arrangement of activity set up before starting your day, you risk escaping center and diverted. An arrangement of activity, built up the prior night is a plan for progress for the next day. You comprehend what your following stages are and what your objectives for the days should be. You work constantly toward that exertion, perceiving that once you're done, objectives (expansive or little) are accomplished and you can proceed onward to the following undertaking for your business.

- Delineating ventures

Influencing a layout of activities to will enable the work at home individual to make more gainful utilization of their days and boost usage of their

time. So as to see a more generative day, it's extraordinary in any case a blueprint and work from it. Right off the bat, list where you need the final product of the venture to be. From that point, work in reverse and detail the means that it will take to arrive. From that point onward, close the framework with the opening move of the task and the conceptualizing idea(s) that were utilized to start the undertaking from the beginning. When you work thusly, you're fundamentally lessening huge tasks to littler, reasonable sorts to get comes about. Work slower, more deliberately and warily to abstain from making mistakes.

- Plan around disturbances

Disturbances have a tendency to occur in identifiable examples with a large portion of them happening at a young hour in the day versus later in the day. Disturbances are

never convenient nor do they "pick" an opportunity to happen. Plan for greater undertakings for later in the day and later in the week when there has a tendency to be less disturbances.

- Allot due dates

Due dates move people to activity and obtain speedy outcomes. Without due dates, matters essentially get proficient when they get refined with no flurry behind them. Influence a due date and you'll to be moved to activity.

Avoid Interruptions

Summation

Huge numbers of the interruptions we bargain as net business visionaries might be killed with a little concentration and assurance. One approach to obtain better control is to use a log to record each occasion of intrusions. To do this, record the going with information into 6 segments:

Follow along

1. Date

Record the date of the disturbance. Keep a log of this similarly as you would client and customer connections and any extra kind of correspondence that you'd esteem pivotal. This will enable you when you to allude back to it for extra information.

2. Time

A ton of times, your days are busier than others similarly as specific circumstances of the day are busier than others. It won't not be possible for you to accept specific calls at specific circumstances of the day rather than different circumstances of the day. Record the time that you accept the disturbance call, in order to take note of any creating examples, plans, et cetera.

You may similarly wish to record the time in any computerized items that you may have which will make less complex for future referencing and documenting. Give careful consideration to designs creating amid a set time of day, week, et cetera.

3. Who

On the off chance that it's another call from grandma, log it. In the event that it's another call from the telephone advertisers, document that as well. Perceive and log who's calling you and irritating your work day.

Are there any rehash miscreants? You may wish to observe this and adjust your timetable as needs be to counteract them.

4.   What

Note what kind of information the call is about. Is it business related at all or essentially plain jabber? This might be and normally is the place the majority of the time wasters are found. Amid business hours is an ideal opportunity to talk over... business!!

Work at home enterprisers are habitually the heartbreaking casualties of accepting that they're not working since they're at home.

Interruption calls will sometimes be senseless calls like formula demands, calls to "vent" or unwarranted babble. Comprehend and record what the discussion was about.

5.   Duration

To what extent are the calls enduring? Two or three minutes all over won't not hurt, but rather may include rapidly! Be solid yet delicate when you're attempting to end your intrusion calls that are pointless for your business.

6. Rating

Rate the call in light of the past 6 factors alongside a reviewing scale like this:

A=essential B=significant C=little esteem D=no esteem

Plan to record this information for about seven days to get an exact measure of what is really happening. On the off chance that it was justified regardless of your while, rate either high or low in view of your tastes. This will help you to better learn where your opportunity goes and how it's being utilized.

After you've amassed this information for seven days, backpedal and add up to up the majority of the A's, B's,

C's, and D's to see where you need to rectify things. Most people locate that over half of their interruptions were C's and D's and were matters that weren't justified regardless of the time spent.

After this, look at every C and D interruption and perceive how they may have been kept away from. Find a way to make sure that it won't rehash itself later on. Do this especially for the dreary disturbances.

A ton of times, people will come to you for data that they may have found themselves.

To cure this, demonstrate to this individual generally accepted methods to discover the data themselves or they'll keep on disrupting you to get it. It's less demanding for them along these lines, yet more troublesome for you and your accessible time. Demonstrate to them industry standards to get what they require without anyone else.

Prioritizing

Summation

Not everything in life can be a need. Numerous vital things will go after consideration over your lifetime, yet there are insufficient hours in anyone's lifetime to offer regard for everything that could conceivably be a need.

Deciding your essential needs is a key exercise in pushing toward more proficient utilization of your chance. Your essential needs give a way to setting aside a few minutes decisions, helping you choose where it is critical to contribute yourself and where you can give up.

Organizing

Setting needs involves choosing what is imperative. For this situation, "vital" means huge to you. What exercises and parts give your life meaning? These are the parts of your life where you might want to succeed the most.

Not everything in your life can be a need. Numerous vital things will vie for consideration over your lifetime, yet there are insufficient hours in anyone's lifetime to offer thoughtfulness regarding everything that could conceivably be a need. Deciding your essential needs is a key exercise in pushing toward more productive utilization of your opportunity.

Your essential needs give a way to setting aside a few minutes decisions, helping you choose where it is imperative to contribute yourself and where you can give up.

Once a day, you likewise need to figure out how to set undertaking needs. Organizing assignments incorporates two stages:

- Recognizing what should be finished

- Deciding on the request in which to do the errands

How would you figure out what function should be finished? Generally, it relates back to your essential needs. To be effective in your opportunity utilize, you need to weed out the work that does not fit with your essential needs. Figure out how to state "no" to employments that look intriguing and may even give a protected feeling of achievement yet don't fit with your essential needs.

You likewise must have the capacity to isolate out the undertakings that require busywork that has a tendency to destroy your opportunity. Numerous assignments that fill your day may not by any means require doing at all or should be possible less every now and again. Errand organizing implies taking a shot at the most noteworthy undertakings first in any case how enticed you are to less critical assignments off the beaten path.

Certain aptitudes help in utilizing time adequately. The vast majority of these abilities are mental. While it isn't important to build up the greater part of the aptitudes, each adds to your capacity to coordinate time use.

Time sense is the aptitude of assessing to what extent an assignment will take to achieve. A decent feeling of time will enable you to be more practical in arranging your exercises. It keeps the disappointment of never having sufficiently very time to achieve undertakings.

To build your opportunity sense, start by giving careful consideration of to what extent it really takes to do certain standard undertakings like preparing toward the beginning of the day, running a heap of clothing or conveying your kid crosswise over town to baseball hone.

Objective setting is the ability of choosing where you need to be toward the finish of a particular time. Objective setting provides guidance to your morning, your day, your week and your lifetime. The activity on choosing your lifetime needs is a type of objective setting. Figure out how to record your objectives.

In the event that you resemble a great many people, objectives are simply wishes until the point that you record them. Keep your objectives particular, as in "weed the bloom beds before the house" as opposed to "take a shot at the yard." Keep your objectives practical or you will ceaselessly be baffled by a feeling of disappointment.

Standard moving is altering your gauges as conditions change. Your benchmarks are what you use to judge in the case of something is adequate, sufficiently clean, really enough, done all around ok.

Fussbudgets have high, inflexible benchmarks, and they experience difficulty acclimating to the changing requests or conditions of their life.

Build up the capacity to move guidelines so you can be happy with not as much as impeccable when your opportunity requests are high, rather than feeling as though you are some way or another missing the mark.

Time preparing of time the work you should be done in a particular period. Now and then time arranging is as basic as working out a schedule to ease you mind from clutching excessively detail.

At especially upsetting circumstances, the schedule may extend to incorporate a more particular timetable of when errands will be finished. While a definite time calendar can be excessively restricting, making it impossible to utilize constantly, it is a decent method to take the weight off at outstandingly requesting circumstances.

Perceiving tarrying is an expertise in itself since slowpokes can complete an extraordinary activity of concealing their stalling from themselves. Stalling is unnecessarily putting off choices or activities.

You may mask the delaying reaction with a reason like sitting tight for motivation, or requiring a vast square of time to think with your complete consideration, or requiring more data previously handling an undertaking.

It takes aptitude to separate between stalling pardons and honest to goodness explanations behind deferring a choice or activity. Without the capacity to perceive when you are, delaying there is minimal possibility of conquering this immobilizing propensity.

Tips to Help You Prioritize

Summation

Here are a few hints to enable you to organize. It is vital to utilize these tips all the time to help stay centered. Every one of these strategies can help you in getting nearer to your objective of ending up more powerful with your chance.

Tips

Every one of these systems can help you in getting nearer to your objective of ending up more compelling with your chance:

1.   Assume responsibility for time

Most people would be astonished in the event that some person came to in their wallet without asking and grabbed the cash found there. Yet, how extraordinary is that from giving other individuals a chance to grab your opportunity? Claim your own particular time and don't enable other individuals to make duties of your chance without your consent. It isn't childish to shield other individuals from expending your opportunity. Give your chance unreservedly when you need however don't make the mix-up of underestimating this asset, or feeling regretful when you don't enable other individuals to squander it. Think about a period of late when some person squandered your opportunity. How might you have managed the circumstance better?

2.   Prioritize

Constantly take a look at yourself to see that you're taking a shot at the most significant things. Helping your youngster talk through an issue, he/she is having or examining the day's occasions with a life partner or companion might be more critical than completing the dishes or a heap of clothing finished. Try not to consider needs just as errands that need doing. As you remind yourself to guide yourself to the most critical undertakings to begin with, you will wind up relinquishing errands that truly did not should be done in any case.

3.   Learn to state "no"

It isn't that adage the word is so troublesome. It's progressively the sentiment coerce that numerous ladies encounter when they utilize the word. Have a go at fixating on the huge things that will be done on the grounds that you utilized that two-letter word to decrease something which was not a piece of your needs. Thinking about your previous week, what are a few things you ought to have said "no" to?

4.   Protect your squares

Think about your day as various vast pieces of time with the squares isolated by characteristic intrusions. Where you have control, keep your squares entire, booking arrangements and gatherings, running errands toward the start or end of a piece rather than in the center. Having an arrangement amidst a square leaves brief period at either end to handle a noteworthy bit of work. Keeping your squares of time as large as conceivable gives you a sentiment having additional time that is accessible.

5.   Delegate

There is that "D" word. Designating implies allocating the obligation regarding an assignment to another person. That implies you never again need to do the undertaking, nor do you need to remind another person to do it. Having the capacity to designate a few errands is a method for arranging for some of your chance for the employments that lone you can do. As another person figures out how to carry out a vocation, don't be enticed to assume control in the event that they are not doing it very right. You need to discover that "done" might be "sufficient."

6.   Think as far as purchasing time

There's a cozy connection amongst time and cash, where one can frequently be substituted for the other. The more chaotic your timetable, the more sensible it is to purchase time by choosing merchandise and ventures that spare you from contributing time. Paying some individual to cut your yard or transport your children to baseball rehearse are cases of buying time. What are a portion of the extra ways you can or do get some time?

7. Learn to work with your natural clock

Individuals have a pinnacle time of day when their vitality is at its most astounding and focus taking care of business. Figure out which time of day is your pinnacle execution time and plan your work as needs be. Keep gatherings and routine undertakings for different parts of the day when you have the decision. What part of the day is best for you to do an undertaking that takes genuine focus?

8. Break down challenging tasks into reasonable pieces

One of the wellsprings of tarrying is that a few assignments can appear to be excessively overpowering, making it impossible to try and start.

Figure out how to separate a vast errand into reasonable pieces and after that start with a piece you know you can deal with. The most difficult advance on real endeavors is frequently the first. Also, you will have a more noteworthy feeling of fulfillment as you finish every individual part of the errand and this can keep you spurred to the end. Think about a noteworthy errand you have in front of you.

How might you separate it into sensible pieces?

9.   Work on defeating lingering

When you perceive that you are dawdling, the subsequent stage is to start beating this time-squandering propensity. Likewise, lingering is a propensity, a routine method for managing undertakings you find tacky or that make you frightful of disappointment. When you see that you are dawdling, make a meeting with yourself to venture out finishing the undertaking. Decide precisely what that initial step will be and after that set a particular time soon to start the work.

10. Reward yourself

Celebrate when a noteworthy assignment is finished or a noteworthy test is met. One of the issues with a boisterous life is that you can be busy to the point that you neglect to see the consummation of a noteworthy bit of work. You simply proceed onward to the following occupation without praising your past progress.

This disappointment prompts concentrating on what is still left fixed as opposed to getting a charge out of what has just been expert. Set up a reward framework for yourself that fills in as both an inspiration to complete certain troublesome assignments and an affirmation that you are making powerful utilization of your chance. Be it an air pocket shower, two parts in your new book, or a telephone call to a companion, recognize your achievement by compensating yourself.

Tips for Staying Focused

Summation

Some may state it is on account of we don't have the fundamental resolve to achieve what we set out to do. Some say it is on account of we are excessively occupied or excessively overpowered, making it impossible, making it impossible to make a move on our determination. My figure is it could be any of those things, yet it is more probable that you have recently begun down a way without your compass and you have begun to lose your direction.

Instead of rattling off a rundown of things, you "should" improve the situation whatever reason, take a seat and consider what it is you truly need to accomplish and set a strong expectation for achieving your objective. I additionally recommend that you center around just a single or two goals at any given moment. Regardless of what it is that you might want to accomplish, setting an expectation can and will set you on a course for progress.

Tips for Staying Focused

Some may state it is on the grounds that we don't have the vital self control to achieve what we set out to do. Some say it is on the grounds that we are excessively occupied or excessively overpowered, making it impossible, making it impossible to make a move on our determination. My figure is it could be any of those things, however it is more probable that you have recently begun down a way without your compass and you have begun to lose your direction.

Instead of rattling off a rundown of things, you "should" improve the situation whatever reason, take a seat and consider what it is you truly need to accomplish and set a strong expectation for achieving your objective. I additionally propose that you center around just a single or two aims at any given moment. Regardless of what it is that you might want to accomplish, setting an aim can and will set you on a course for progress.

Here are 5 top tips to at last accomplishing your objective:

Tip 1 Get clear. In setting a goal, you're influencing it to clear to yourself and to other individuals precisely what you intend to do. Characterize the meaning of what achieving your objective would be. For example, you know you've achieved your objective of enhancing your administration aptitudes when you reliably feel more happy with your capacity to manage extreme circumstances and propel your staff. You may even understand that advancement you have been after!

Tip 2 Realize that an aim comes in a few sizes and each expansive objective is loaded with aims of all shapes and sizes. With complete, every expectation will eventually prompt achievement. For example, if your determination is to enhance your administration abilities, your first aim

might be to talk with your organization to discover what abilities and qualities you might need to center around.

Tip 3 don't give disarray a chance to overpower your aim. You may have heaps of enthusiasm about your determination, however enthusiasm without an arrangement is squandered vitality and will in the long run fail out. Setting a goal to make a stride towards your objective every day will keep you on the correct way and help to gather up perplexity.

Tip 4 Use your assets. Request what you need and need from other individuals. When you unmistakably express your aim and your demand of other individuals, you have the chance to pick up an accomplice and a cheering area. For example, on the off chance that you admire some individual's administration style, approach him or her for tips and potentially even help. Odds are they will be complimented and extremely ready to share counsel.

Tip 5 Be responsible. Pick your resolutions precisely by choosing what truly interests you. You may request that some person you trust help keep you responsible. By the by, nothing can replace regarding your aims to yourself. You will be astounded at how your confidence and feeling of achievement will increment when you accomplish your objectives.

Work Less Accomplish More

Abstract

On the off chance that you are feeling exhausted, overpowered or out and out finished it, the accompanying time-administration tips can enable you to expand your profitability so you can achieve more.

Work Less Accomplish More

In the event that you are feeling exhausted, overpowered or out and out finished it, the accompanying time-administration tips can enable you to boost your profitability so you can achieve more.

Isolate Work from Home

Between reacting to individual messages, texting and handling wireless calls from your children, it can get hard to remain concentrated on the undertakings. Subsequently, when you're in the workplace attempt to focus on you function however much as could reasonably be expected. At that point when you're at home, you can truly manage your issues there without diversion. You'll end up having better quality time the two spots. Isolating your work obligations from home-related ones will enable you to keep your psyche on work when you're there and, thusly, hesitate less, believe less overpowered and achieve more.

Build up limits and stay with them

While it is constantly awesome to endeavor to make everyone cheerful constantly, it is simply impractical in a work environment led by the unquestionable laws of time and space. Realize when to state no. There are times when it's entitlement to go past the obligation at hand at work. For Instance, when it is a genuine crisis, at that point I wouldn't fret remaining late or putting it all out there.

In any case, that is not the same as simply giving individuals a chance to dump their very late work around your work area so they can make it home early.

While you have to do your work, you additionally need to deal with yourself and know your activity's limits.

Get Organized

Time spent chasing for documents or lost telephone numbers could be utilized for gaining ground on your daily agenda. Great authoritative structures are basic in whenever administration design. Spend a couple of minutes toward the finish of regular noting phone messages, and messages. It generally is sorted out and not given messages a chance to heap up. It will dependably spare you time. Sticky notes posted on your console can enable you to recall the most vital assignment that should be done for the duration of the day.

Everybody has their own particular framework for being composed. Attempt these tips. They may simply add two or three minutes to your day alongside you routine you as of now hone.

Set aside a few minutes for Yourself

Any very much built plan for the day needs to incorporate some time for unwinding and focusing yourself, or you may twist up excessively worried, making it impossible to benefit anyone in any way.

Diligent work = Resistance and is the inverse of stream.

For one thing, nobody likes to "need to" do anything. When you say I "need to" pay my bills, so I "need to" strive to get the cash. As of now you can detect the gloom and weakness in the general concept of "having to" accomplish something you normally stand up to. When you "need to" do anything, you're in a condition of protection. You are battling the common stream by pointing yourself upstream, standing up to. Following a couple of many years of this protection, you can perceive how a few people in the long run burnout, lose their point of view, lose delight, make disorder and at last lose life itself. No, working hard to get what we need isn't the appropriate response. Crushing without end at something is the underlying driver of all failure throughout everyday life. Turn this thought around.

Find and seek after your easiest course of action.

What do you cherish? I mean truly cherish! What do you get a kick out of the chance to "play at"? What are you easily great at? What movement energizes you to a degree that when you're occupied with it, you really lose your familiarity with time? Consider these inquiries profoundly. Inside this thought of "play" is the seed of euphoric, simple, casual, regular, languid creation. There's no working when you're occupied with an action you believe you were destined to do. On the off chance that you have a thought that you want to play with, do you constrain yourself to play with it? Obviously not. You are normally attracted to it. You're affectionately occupied with it. Things are simple. There's no work included and the aftereffects of your creation appear to be nearly paradise sent.

Your entire life must reflect what you're normally attracted to do. It is fundamental to achieving your heart's want. Try not to exchange one all the more second of your valuable life vitality buckling down at accomplishing your objectives. Find your most noteworthy blessings that have been with you since the day you were conceived and utilize them to make an incentive in a basic and loose way! All that you have to make your prosperity is as of now inside you.

Any valuable thought that has lifted the educational experience of people has come to fruition since individuals might want to abstain from doing diligent work. Every one of our developments all through history have been made to improve life simpler and. Diligent work is counter-beneficial to the heading of development and life extending. Diligent work close off the stream of inventive, enlivened vitality. Diligent work isn't in arrangement with the

laws of creation. You're made of a similar stuff and this regular law applies to you wittingly or accidentally. You'll never wind up solid, well off and insightful:

- keeping your nose to the grindstone

- pushing the ball tough

- working your fingers deep down

- going to a salt mine

- spending the day with a slave driver

There's a less demanding, apathetic, do nothing approach to make the life you have constantly wanted. You should draw in yourself in what you cherish, play and mess around with. Play with everything. On the off chance that it isn't fun, and feels like diligent work, you're diminishing your potential for making enormous achievement in your life. Adjust your concentration and regard for just that which you adore.

At that point discover accomplices who adore doing the exercises you oppose doing. When you set up everything together, you will take a quantum jump in your energy to make what you want.

Using Affirmations

Abstract

In the event that you utilize confirmations, make it a point to utilize them every now and again and don't quit utilizing them regardless of whether your circumstance is showing signs of improvement. The more you utilize confirmations, the better the circumstance. There are attestations for each sort of circumstance; needs, lingering, center, and quietness are only a couple. Here are a few attestations that may help you all through you day.

Attestations

On the off chance that you utilize certifications, make it a point to utilize them as often as possible and don't quit utilizing them regardless of whether your circumstance is showing signs of improvement. The more you utilize confirmations, the better the circumstance. There are assertions for each kind of circumstance; needs, stalling, center, and tranquility are only a couple. Here are a few assertions that may help you all through you day.

Organizing

•   I am qualified for carry on with a quiet life, brimming with euphoria and request.

•   I set practical objectives, recollecting that my first need is myself.

•   I plan errands at the correct pace for me.

•   I proactively choose what undertakings I ought to do first and which are more essential.

•   I take something off my timetable before I include one.

•   I set aside a few minutes for anything new that I bring into my life.

- I discover no compelling reason to accumulate my opportunity on one particular thing.

- I am ready to appoint the assignments that I can't - or ought not - be doing.

- I set aside a few minutes for play and rest and don't enable myself to work relentless.

- I acknowledge my advance since it is at my own pace.

- I realize that my understanding, resilience, and endeavors enable me to learn and develop to be a more grounded adaptation of me.

- I am delicate with my endeavors, realizing that my better approach for living requires much practice and tolerance.

Delaying

- I make the move and surrender the result over to God.

- There is no attempt, just do.

- My want to get on with things is more grounded than my want to delay.

- Procrastination is my foe.

- I make a move towards my objectives every day.

- I appreciate the achievement of completing an assignment.

- I begin this assignment with a little, defective advance. I will feel awesome and have a lot of time for play!

- I anticipate completing things.

- Among all that I do I adore working the most.

Core interest

- I am alarm and mindful constantly.

- I am constantly centered around what I am doing.

- I am mindful and perceptive consistently.

- I am mindful and display consistently.

- I am quiet and centered in all that I do.

- I am totally caught up right now.

- I am totally centered around what I am doing.

- I am effortlessly consumed by all that I do.

- I am entranced and engaged with each undertaking I perform.

- I am engaged and loose in all that I do.

- I am completely engaged and exhibit in all connections with others.

Quietness

- I have Peace of brain constantly.

- No matter what I am looked with I will try to avoid panicking.

- I have internal peace.

- My mind is dependably in a quiet cherishing place.

Conclusion

Make things as simple as could reasonably be expected. This implies streamlining methodology and influencing things to work simpler. For instance, in the event that you assume praise cards in your business, make that more accessible than dealing with watches that must be conveyed to the bank, got the money for and additionally kept. In the event that there are ventures to a technique that might be wiped out, do that and watch your efficiency zoom.

The more you improve, the less complex it will be for your business to run. Things and techniques run smoother with less advances and decline the conceivable outcomes of slip-ups.

Disentanglement is an incredible apparatus for discovering additional time.

Too, utilize utilizing. The idea of utilizing alludes to getting and using numerous assets of things out of materials you've just made. In spite of the fact that it might take a specific measure of expertise and imagination to do this well, in the whole deal it might pay off twofold times in esteem.

When you start utilizing, you may fundamentally increase your profits from a one-time speculation of your work. In creating new materials for your business, constantly ask yourself, "How may I use this once more?"

By and large, when we gain ground in life it is on the grounds that life goes ahead us to advance. Sometimes is it as our very own result cognizant decision and activity. Over the long course of our lives, such constrained progression happens in eccentric routes, in some cases through upbeat, however frequently through troubled encounters. Without a doubt, this isn't the best method to advance throughout everyday life.

However that is the way the lion's share of us advance throughout everyday life. We call such wasteful, unusual, life-winding advancement.

Be that as it may, with this book and these tips we can deliberately change our conduct without the additional pressure.

We can have adjust and accomplishment throughout everyday life. What's more, we can get our needs in line and keep them there. What is preventing you from snatching those additional minutes and hours in your day? The main answer is, you! So escape your direction and begin achieving more by doing less!

Thanks again for buying my book. If you have a minute, please leave a positive review. You can leave your review by clicking on this link:

Leave your review here. Thank you!

I take reviews seriously and always look at them. This way, you are helping me provide you better content that you will LOVE in the future. A review doesn't have to be long, just one or two sentences and a number of stars you find appropriate (hopefully 5 of course).

Also, if I think your review is useful, I will mark it as "helpful." This will help you become more known on Amazon as a decent reviewer, and will ensure that more authors will contact you with free e-books in the future. This is how we can help each other.

DISCLAIMER: This information is provided "as is." The author, publishers and/or marketers of this information disclaim any loss or liability, either directly or indirectly as a consequence of applying the information presented herein, or in regard to the use and application of said information. No guarantee is given, either expressed or implied, in regard to the merchantability, accuracy, or acceptability of the information. The pages within this e-book have been copyrighted.